2022-2023

Monthly Planner

This Planner Belongs To:

_____

_____

EightIdd Ge.Press

Want FREEBIES?

Email Us At:

eightidd@gmail.com

Title the email "**2022 Planner**" and let us know that you purchased our planner.

THANKS FOR YOUR AMAZING SUPPORT!

>>>>>>>>>>>>>>>>>>>>>>>>>>>>>>>>

For Enquiries and Customer Service email us at:

eightidd@gmail.com

2022 CALENDAR

January

S	M	T	W	T	F	S
						1
2	3	4	5	6	7	8
9	10	11	12	13	14	15
16	17	18	19	20	21	22
23	24	25	26	27	28	29
30	31					

February

S	M	T	W	T	F	S
		1	2	3	4	5
6	7	8	9	10	11	12
13	14	15	16	17	18	19
20	21	22	23	24	25	26
27	28					

March

S	M	T	W	T	F	S
		1	2	3	4	5
6	7	8	9	10	11	12
13	14	15	16	17	18	19
20	21	22	23	24	25	26
27	28	29	30	31		

April

S	M	T	W	T	F	S
					1	2
3	4	5	6	7	8	9
10	11	12	13	14	15	16
17	18	19	20	21	22	23
24	25	26	27	28	29	30

May

S	M	T	W	T	F	S
1	2	3	4	5	6	7
8	9	10	11	12	13	14
15	16	17	18	19	20	21
22	23	24	25	26	27	28
29	30	31				

June

S	M	T	W	T	F	S
			1	2	3	4
5	6	7	8	9	10	11
12	13	14	15	16	17	18
19	20	21	22	23	24	25
26	27	28	29	30		

July

S	M	T	W	T	F	S
					1	2
3	4	5	6	7	8	9
10	11	12	13	14	15	16
17	18	19	20	21	22	23
24	25	26	27	28	29	30
31						

August

S	M	T	W	T	F	S
	1	2	3	4	5	6
7	8	9	10	11	12	13
14	15	16	17	18	19	20
21	22	23	24	25	26	27
28	29	30	31			

September

S	M	T	W	T	F	S
				1	2	3
4	5	6	7	8	9	10
11	12	13	14	15	16	17
18	19	20	21	22	23	24
25	26	27	28	29	30	

October

S	M	T	W	T	F	S
						1
2	3	4	5	6	7	8
9	10	11	12	13	14	15
16	17	18	19	20	21	22
23	24	25	26	27	28	29
30	31					

November

S	M	T	W	T	F	S
		1	2	3	4	5
6	7	8	9	10	11	12
13	14	15	16	17	18	19
20	21	22	23	24	25	26
27	28	29	30			

December

S	M	T	W	T	F	S
				1	2	3
4	5	6	7	8	9	10
11	12	13	14	15	16	17
18	19	20	21	22	23	24
25	26	27	28	29	30	31

UNITED STATES 2022 HOLIDAYS

January 1, 2022	Saturday	New Year's Day
January 17, 2022	Monday	Martin Luther King Jr. Day
February 14, 2022	Monday	Valentine's Day
February 21, 2022	Monday	Washington's Birthday
April 18, 2022	Monday	Tax Day
April 27, 2022	Wednesday	Administrative Professionals Day
May 8, 2022	Sunday	Mother's Day
May 30, 2022	Monday	Memorial Day
June 19, 2022	Sunday	Father's Day
July 4, 2022	Monday	Independence Day
September 5, 2022	Monday	Labor Day
October 10, 2022	Monday	Columbus Day
October 31, 2022	Monday	Halloween
November 11, 2022	Friday	Veterans Day
November 24, 2022	Thursday	Thanksgiving Day
November 25, 2022	Friday	Day after Thanksgiving Day
December 24, 2022	Saturday	Christmas Eve
December 25, 2022	Sunday	Christmas Day
December 26, 2022	Monday	Christmas Day (substitute day)
December 31, 2022	Saturday	New Year's Eve

NOTES:

BIRTHDAYS 2022

January:

February:

March:

April:

May:

June:

July:

August:

September:

October:

November:

December:

JANUARY 2022

_____
_____
_____

Sunday	Monday	Tuesday	Wednesday
2	3	4	5
9	10	11	12
16	17 Martin Luther King Jr. Day	18	19
23 / 30	24 / 31	25	26

Favorite Quote

Priorities

Thursday	Friday	Saturday	To-do
		1 New Year's Day	
6	7	8	
13	14	15	
20	21	22	
27	28	29	

Notes

NOTES - PROJECTS - GOALS

NOTES - PROJECTS - GOALS

FEBRUARY 2022

Sunday	Monday	Tuesday	Wednesday
		1	2
6	7	8	9
13	14 Valentine'sDay	15	16
20	21 Presidents'Day	22	23
27	28		

Favorite Quote

Thursday	Friday	Saturday	To-do
3	4	5	☐ _____
			☐ _____
			☐ _____
			☐ _____
10	11	12	☐ _____
			☐ _____
			☐ _____
			☐ _____
17	18	19	☐ _____
			☐ _____
			☐ _____
			☐ _____
24	25	26	

Notes

_____
_____
_____
_____
_____
_____
_____
_____

NOTES - PROJECTS - GOALS

NOTES - PROJECTS - GOALS

MARCH 2022

Sunday	Monday	Tuesday	Wednesday
		1	2
6	7	8	9
13	14	15	16
20	21	22	23
27	28	29	30

Priorities

Thursday	Friday	Saturday	To-do
3	4	5	☐ _____
			☐ _____
			☐ _____
			☐ _____
10	11	12	☐ _____
			☐ _____
			☐ _____
			☐ _____
17	18	19	☐ _____
			☐ _____
			☐ _____
24	25	26	☐ _____
31			

Notes

_____

_____

_____

_____

_____

_____

_____

_____

NOTES - PROJECTS - GOALS

NOTES - PROJECTS - GOALS

APRIL 2022

_____
_____
_____

Sunday	Monday	Tuesday	Wednesday
3	4	5	6
10	11	12	13
17 Easter Sunday	18 Tax Day	19	20
24	25	26	27

Favorite Quote

Thursday	Friday	Saturday
	1	2
7	8	9
14	15	16
	Good Friday	
21	22	23
	Earth Day	
28	29	30

To-do

- ☐ _____
- ☐ _____
- ☐ _____
- ☐ _____
- ☐ _____
- ☐ _____
- ☐ _____
- ☐ _____
- ☐ _____
- ☐ _____
- ☐ _____
- ☐ _____

Notes

_____
_____
_____
_____
_____
_____
_____
_____

NOTES - PROJECTS - GOALS

NOTES - PROJECTS - GOALS

MAY 2022

_____
_____
_____

Sunday	Monday	Tuesday	Wednesday
1	2	3	4
8 Mother'sDay	9	10	11
15	16	17	18
22	23	24	25
29	30 Memorial Day	31	

Favorite Quote

Priorities

Thursday	Friday	Saturday	To-do
5 Cinco de Mayo	6	7	☐ _____ ☐ _____ ☐ _____ ☐ _____ ☐ _____
12	13	14	☐ _____ ☐ _____ ☐ _____ ☐ _____ ☐ _____
19	20	21	☐ _____ ☐ _____
26	27	28	

Notes

_____
_____
_____
_____
_____
_____
_____
_____

NOTES - PROJECTS - GOALS

NOTES - PROJECTS - GOALS

JUNE 2022

Sunday	Monday	Tuesday	Wednesday
			1
5	6	7	8
12	13	14 Flag Day	15
19 Father'sDay	20	21	22
26	27	28	29

Priorities

Thursday	Friday	Saturday	To-do
2	3	4	
9	10	11	
16	17	18	
23	24	25	
30			

To-do

- ☐ _____
- ☐ _____
- ☐ _____
- ☐ _____
- ☐ _____
- ☐ _____
- ☐ _____
- ☐ _____
- ☐ _____
- ☐ _____
- ☐ _____
- ☐ _____

Notes

_____
_____
_____
_____
_____
_____
_____
_____
_____
_____

NOTES - PROJECTS - GOALS

NOTES - PROJECTS - GOALS

JULY 2022

_____
_____
_____

Sunday	Monday	Tuesday	Wednesday
3	4 Independence Day	5	6
10	11	12	13
17	18	19	20
24 31	25	26	27

Priorities

Thursday	Friday	Saturday	To-do
	1	2	
7	8	9	
14	15	16	
21	22	23	
28	29	30	

Notes

NOTES - PROJECTS - GOALS

NOTES - PROJECTS - GOALS

AUGUST 2022

_____
_____
_____

Sunday	Monday	Tuesday	Wednesday
	1	2	3
7	8	9	10
14	15	16	17
21	22	23	24
28	29	30	31

Priorities

Thursday	Friday	Saturday	To-do
4	5	6	☐ _____
			☐ _____
			☐ _____
			☐ _____
			☐ _____
11	12	13	☐ _____
			☐ _____
			☐ _____
			☐ _____
			☐ _____
18	19	20	☐ _____
			☐ _____
25	26	27	Notes

Notes

_____

_____

_____

_____

_____

_____

_____

_____

NOTES - PROJECTS - GOALS

NOTES - PROJECTS - GOALS

SEPTEMBER 2022

Sunday	Monday	Tuesday	Wednesday
4	5 Labor Day	6	7
11	12	13	14
18	19	20	21
25	26	27	28

Priorities

Thursday	Friday	Saturday	To-do
1	2	3	☐ _____
			☐ _____
			☐ _____
			☐ _____
			☐ _____
8	9	10	☐ _____
			☐ _____
			☐ _____
			☐ _____
			☐ _____
15	16	17	☐ _____
			☐ _____
			☐ _____
22	23	24	
29	30		

Notes

_____
_____
_____
_____
_____
_____
_____

NOTES - PROJECTS - GOALS

NOTES - PROJECTS - GOALS

OCTOBER 2022

Sunday	Monday	Tuesday	Wednesday
2	3	4	5
9	10 Columbus Day	11	12
16	17	18	19
23 / 30	24 / 31 Halloween	25	26

Favorite Quote

Priorities

Thursday	Friday	Saturday	To-do
		1	☐ _____
			☐ _____
			☐ _____
			☐ _____
			☐ _____
6	7	8	☐ _____
			☐ _____
			☐ _____
			☐ _____
			☐ _____
13	14	15	☐ _____
			☐ _____
20	21	22	
27	28	29	

Notes

_____
_____
_____
_____
_____
_____
_____
_____

NOTES - PROJECTS - GOALS

NOTES - PROJECTS - GOALS

NOVEMBER 2022

_____
_____
_____

Sunday	Monday	Tuesday	Wednesday
		1	2
6	7	8	9
13	14	15	16
20	21	22	23
27	28	29	30

Favorite Quote

Priorities

Thursday	Friday	Saturday	To-do
3	4	5	☐ _____
			☐ _____
			☐ _____
10	11	12	☐ _____
			☐ _____
	Veterans Day		☐ _____
17	18	19	☐ _____
			☐ _____
			☐ _____
24	25	26	☐ _____
			☐ _____
Thanksgiving Day	Black Friday		☐ _____

Notes

_____

_____

_____

_____

_____

_____

_____

_____

_____

NOTES - PROJECTS - GOALS

NOTES - PROJECTS - GOALS

DECEMBER 2022

_____
_____
_____

Sunday	Monday	Tuesday	Wednesday
4	5	6	7
11	12	13	14
18	19	20	21
25 Christmas Day	26 Boxing Day	27	28

Favorite Quote

Priorities

Thursday	Friday	Saturday
1	2	3
8	9	10
15	16	17
22	23	24 Christmas Eve
29	30	31 New Year's Eve

To-do

☐ _____
☐ _____
☐ _____
☐ _____
☐ _____
☐ _____
☐ _____
☐ _____
☐ _____
☐ _____
☐ _____
☐ _____

Notes

NOTES - PROJECTS - GOALS

NOTES - PROJECTS - GOALS

2023 CALENDAR

January

S	M	T	W	T	F	S
1	2	3	4	5	6	7
8	9	10	11	12	13	14
15	16	17	18	19	20	21
22	23	24	25	26	27	28
29	30	31				

February

S	M	T	W	T	F	S
			1	2	3	4
5	6	7	8	9	10	11
12	13	14	15	16	17	18
19	20	21	22	23	24	25
26	27	28				

March

S	M	T	W	T	F	S
			1	2	3	4
5	6	7	8	9	10	11
12	13	14	15	16	17	18
19	20	21	22	23	24	25
26	27	28	29	30	31	

April

S	M	T	W	T	F	S
						1
2	3	4	5	6	7	8
9	10	11	12	13	14	15
16	17	18	19	20	21	22
23	24	25	26	27	28	29
30						

May

S	M	T	W	T	F	S
	1	2	3	4	5	6
7	8	9	10	11	12	13
14	15	16	17	18	19	20
21	22	23	24	25	26	27
28	29	30	31			

June

S	M	T	W	T	F	S
				1	2	3
4	5	6	7	8	9	10
11	12	13	14	15	16	17
18	19	20	21	22	23	24
25	26	27	28	29	30	

July

S	M	T	W	T	F	S
						1
2	3	4	5	6	7	8
9	10	11	12	13	14	15
16	17	18	19	20	21	22
23	24	25	26	27	28	29
30	31					

August

S	M	T	W	T	F	S
		1	2	3	4	5
6	7	8	9	10	11	12
13	14	15	16	17	18	19
20	21	22	23	24	25	26
27	28	29	30	31		

September

S	M	T	W	T	F	S
					1	2
3	4	5	6	7	8	9
10	11	12	13	14	15	16
17	18	19	20	21	22	23
24	25	26	27	28	29	30

October

S	M	T	W	T	F	S
1	2	3	4	5	6	7
8	9	10	11	12	13	14
15	16	17	18	19	20	21
22	23	24	25	26	27	28
29	30	31				

November

S	M	T	W	T	F	S
			1	2	3	4
5	6	7	8	9	10	11
12	13	14	15	16	17	18
19	20	21	22	23	24	25
26	27	28	29	30		

December

S	M	T	W	T	F	S
					1	2
3	4	5	6	7	8	9
10	11	12	13	14	15	16
17	18	19	20	21	22	23
24	25	26	27	28	29	30
31						

UNITED STATES 2023 HOLIDAYS

January 1, 2023	Sunday	New Year's Day
January 2, 2023	Monday	New Year's Day (substitute day)
January 16, 2023	Monday	Martin Luther King Jr. Day
February 14, 2023	Tuesday	Valentine's Day
February 20, 2023	Monday	Washington's Birthday
April 18, 2023	Tuesday	Tax Day
April 26, 2023	Wednesday	Administrative Professionals Day
May 14, 2023	Sunday	Mother's Day
May 29, 2023	Monday	Memorial Day
June 18, 2023	Sunday	Father's Day
July 4, 2023	Tuesday	Independence Day
September 4, 2023	Monday	Labor Day
October 9, 2023	Monday	Columbus Day
October 31, 2023	Tuesday	Halloween
November 10, 2023	Friday	Veterans Day (substitute day)
November 11, 2023	Saturday	Veterans Day
November 23, 2023	Thursday	Thanksgiving Day
November 24, 2023	Friday	Day after Thanksgiving Day
December 24, 2023	Sunday	Christmas Eve
December 25, 2023	Monday	Christmas Day
December 31, 2023	Sunday	New Year's Eve

NOTES:

BIRTHDAYS 2023

January:

February:

March:

April:

May:

June:

July:

August:

September:

October:

November:

December:

NOTES - PROJECTS - GOALS

JANUARY 2023

Sunday	Monday	Tuesday	Wednesday
1 New Year's Day	2	3	4
8	9	10	11
15	16 Martin Luther King Jr. Day	17	18
22	23	24	25
29	30	31	

Priorities

Thursday	Friday	Saturday	To-do
5	6	7	
12	13	14	
19	20	21	
26	27	28	

Notes

NOTES - PROJECTS - GOALS

NOTES - PROJECTS - GOALS

FEBRUARY 2023

Sunday	Monday	Tuesday	Wednesday
			1
5	6	7	8
12	13	14 Valentine'sDay	15
19	20 Presidents'Day	21	22
26	27	28	

Favorite Quote

Thursday	Friday	Saturday	To-do
2	3	4	☐ _____ ☐ _____ ☐ _____ ☐ _____ ☐ _____
9	10	11	☐ _____ ☐ _____ ☐ _____ ☐ _____ ☐ _____
16	17	18	☐ _____ ☐ _____ ☐ _____
23	24	25	**Notes**

Notes

NOTES - PROJECTS - GOALS

NOTES - PROJECTS - GOALS

MARCH 2023

Sunday	Monday	Tuesday	Wednesday
			1
5	6	7	8
12	13	14	15
19	20	21	22
26	27	28	29

Favorite Quote

Priorities

Thursday	Friday	Saturday	To-do
2	3	4	☐ _____
			☐ _____
			☐ _____
			☐ _____
9	10	11	☐ _____
			☐ _____
			☐ _____
			☐ _____
			☐ _____
16	17	18	☐ _____
			☐ _____
			☐ _____
23	24	25	**Notes**
30	31		

NOTES - PROJECTS - GOALS

NOTES - PROJECTS - GOALS

APPRIL 2023

Sunday	Monday	Tuesday	Wednesday
2	3	4	5
9 Easter Sunday	10 Tax Day	11	12
16	17	18	19
23 / 30	24	25	26

Favorite Quote

Thursday	Friday	Saturday	To-do
		1	
6	7	8	
	Good Friday		
13	14	15	
20	21	22	
		Earth Day	
27	28	29	

Notes

NOTES - PROJECTS - GOALS

NOTES - PROJECTS - GOALS

MAY 2023

_____
_____
_____

Sunday	Monday	Tuesday	Wednesday
	1	2	3
7	8	9	10
14 Mother'sDay	15	16	17
21	22	23	24
28	29 Memorial Day	30	31

Favorite Quote

Priorities

Thursday	Friday	Saturday	To-do
4	5	6	
	Cinco de Mayo		
11	12	13	
18	19	21	
25	26	27	

To-do

☐ _____
☐ _____
☐ _____
☐ _____
☐ _____
☐ _____
☐ _____
☐ _____
☐ _____
☐ _____
☐ _____
☐ _____

Notes

_____
_____
_____
_____
_____
_____
_____
_____
_____
_____

NOTES - PROJECTS - GOALS

NOTES - PROJECTS - GOALS

JUNE 2023

_____
_____
_____

Sunday	Monday	Tuesday	Wednesday
4	5	6	7
11	12	13	14 Flag Day
18 Father'sDay	19	20	21
25	26	27	28

Priorities

Thursday	Friday	Saturday
1	2	3
8	9	10
15	16	17
22	23	24
29	30	

To-do

☐ _____
☐ _____
☐ _____
☐ _____
☐ _____
☐ _____
☐ _____
☐ _____
☐ _____
☐ _____
☐ _____
☐ _____

Notes

NOTES - PROJECTS - GOALS

NOTES - PROJECTS - GOALS

JULY 2023

_____
_____
_____

Sunday	Monday	Tuesday	Wednesday
2	3	4 Independence Day	5
9	10	11	12
16	17	18	19
23 / 30	24 / 31	25	26

Priorities

Thursday	Friday	Saturday	To-do
		1	
6	7	8	
13	14	15	
20	21	22	
27	28	29	

Notes

NOTES - PROJECTS - GOALS

NOTES - PROJECTS - GOALS

AUGUST 2023

Sunday	Monday	Tuesday	Wednesday
		1	2
6	7	8	9
13	14	15	16
20	21	22	23
27	28	29	30

Favorite Quote

Thursday	Friday	Saturday	To-do
3	4	5	☐ _____
			☐ _____
			☐ _____
			☐ _____
10	11	12	☐ _____
			☐ _____
			☐ _____
			☐ _____
17	18	19	☐ _____
			☐ _____
			☐ _____
24	25	26	
31			

Notes

_____
_____
_____
_____
_____
_____
_____

NOTES - PROJECTS - GOALS

NOTES - PROJECTS - GOALS

SEPTEMBER 2023

Sunday	Monday	Tuesday	Wednesday
3	4 Labor Day	5	6
10	11	12	13
17	18	19	20
24	25	26	27

Favorite Quote

Thursday	Friday	Saturday	To-do
	1	2	☐ _____
			☐ _____
			☐ _____
			☐ _____
7	8	9	☐ _____
			☐ _____
			☐ _____
			☐ _____
14	15	16	☐ _____
			☐ _____
			☐ _____
			☐ _____
21	22	23	**Notes**
28	29	30	

NOTES - PROJECTS - GOALS

NOTES - PROJECTS - GOALS

OCTOBER 2023

Sunday	Monday	Tuesday	Wednesday
1	2	3	4
8	9 Columbus Day	10	11
15	16	17	18
22	23	24	25
29	30	31 Halloween	

Priorities

Thursday	Friday	Saturday	To-do
5	6	7	
12	13	14	
19	20	21	
26	27	28	

Notes

NOTES - PROJECTS - GOALS

NOTES - PROJECTS - GOALS

NOVEMBER 2023

Sunday	Monday	Tuesday	Wednesday
			1
5	6	7	8
12	13	14	15
19	20	21	22
26	27	28	29

Favorite Quote

Thursday	Friday	Saturday	To-do
2	3	4	
9	10	11 Veterans Day	
16	17	18	
23 Thanksgiving Day	24 Black Friday	25	
30			

Notes

NOTES - PROJECTS - GOALS

NOTES - PROJECTS - GOALS

DECEMBER 2023

Sunday	Monday	Tuesday	Wednesday
3	4	5	6
10	11	12	13
17	18	19	20
24 Christmas Eve / 31 New Year's Eve	25 Christmas Day	26 Boxing Day	27

Priorities

Thursday

Friday

Saturday

To-do

Thursday	Friday	Saturday
	1	2
7	8	9
14	15	16
21	22	23
28	29	30

☐ _____
☐ _____
☐ _____
☐ _____
☐ _____
☐ _____
☐ _____
☐ _____
☐ _____
☐ _____
☐ _____
☐ _____

Notes

NOTES - PROJECTS - GOALS

NOTES - PROJECTS - GOALS

CONTACTS

CONTACTS

CONTACTS

PASSWORDS

Website	
Username	
Password	
Email	
Notes	

Website	
Username	
Password	
Email	
Notes	

Website	
Username	
Password	
Email	
Notes	

Website	
Username	
Password	
Email	
Notes	

Website	
Username	
Password	
Email	
Notes	

Website	
Username	
Password	
Email	
Notes	

Website	
Username	
Password	
Email	
Notes	

Website	
Username	
Password	
Email	
Notes	

PASSWORDS

Website	
Username	
Password	
Email	
Notes	

Website	
Username	
Password	
Email	
Notes	

Website	
Username	
Password	
Email	
Notes	

Website	
Username	
Password	
Email	
Notes	

Website	
Username	
Password	
Email	
Notes	

Website	
Username	
Password	
Email	
Notes	

Website	
Username	
Password	
Email	
Notes	

Website	
Username	
Password	
Email	
Notes	

PASSWORDS

Website	
Username	
Password	
Email	
Notes	

Website	
Username	
Password	
Email	
Notes	

Website	
Username	
Password	
Email	
Notes	

Website	
Username	
Password	
Email	
Notes	

Website	
Username	
Password	
Email	
Notes	

Website	
Username	
Password	
Email	
Notes	

Website	
Username	
Password	
Email	
Notes	

Website	
Username	
Password	
Email	
Notes	

Made in United States
North Haven, CT
19 May 2022

19219410R00063